MOTHERHOOD:
Nailed It!

Published by Sellers Publishing, Inc.
Copyright © 2020 Sellers Publishing, Inc.

Sellers Publishing, Inc.
161 John Roberts Road, South Portland, Maine 04106
Visit our website: www.sellerspublishing.com • E-mail: rsp@rsvp.com

Charlotte Cromwell, Production Editor
Compiled and designed by Charlotte Cromwell

Cover image credit © 2020 studiostoks/Shutterstock.com;
interior image credits © 2020 studiostoks/Shutterstock.com.

ISBN 13: 978-1-5319-1210-9

10 9 8 7 6 5 4 3 2 1

Printed in China.

MOTHERHOOD:
Nailed It!

humorous perspectives
from moms who get it

SELLERS
PUBLISHING

Having kids makes you look stable to the people who thought you were crazy, and crazy to the people who thought you were stable.

KELLY OXFORD

Sometimes I stand there going, 'I'm not doing any of this right!' And then I get this big man belch out of her and I go, 'Ah, we accomplished this together.'

CHRISTINA APPLEGATE

What a parent's
bucket list looks like:

3. Drink hot coffee

2. Shower without kids
banging on the door

1. Pee alone

I don't know what
I'm doing, but then
I have to remind myself
no parent does, right?

ELLIE KEMPER

No one is more full of [crap] than a parent that just said 'maybe.'

JUST SURVIVING MOTHERHOOD

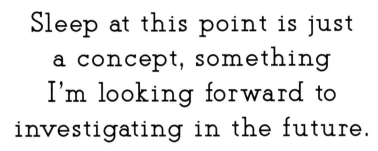

Sleep at this point is just a concept, something I'm looking forward to investigating in the future.

AMY POEHLER

At bed time my children
turn into dehydrated
philosophers who
need a hug.

All parents want is for
our kids to go to bed so
we can watch a show
with bad words in it
and eat the hidden snacks.

SIMON CHOLLAND

Six-year-old: "Mom, can I —"

Me: "You can do anything you want as long as I don't have to get up."

TONI HAMMER

I don't care how cute your kid is. When you wake up in the middle of the night and see them standing next to your bed, they are terrifying.

@MAUGHAMMOM

Parenting is a constant battle between going to bed early to catch up on sleep, or staying up late to get alone time.

UNKNOWN

'It's not about how tired you are, it's about how tired you are making everyone else.' (my husband explaining bedtime to our kids).

HEIDI ST. JOHN

When you have kids, "sleeping in" is just lying in bed trying to figure out what that crash was.

AMY DILLON

section three
Hiding in the bathroom

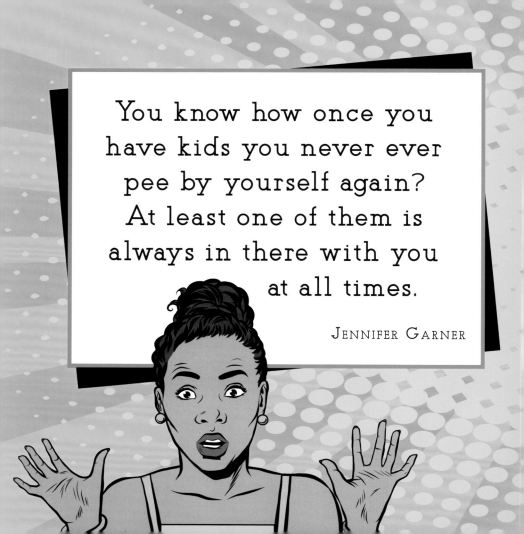

Son: Are you eating pie
for breakfast?

Me (eating pie): No, fruit
casserole. Want some?

Son: NO. I hate casserole.

Me (whispers): I know . . .

KATHRYN LEEHANE

As a parent, there's a lot more yelling at people from the bathroom than I would have imagined.

UNKNOWN

Meditation is my thing. But I'm not going to lie: sometimes I go into my closet and lock the door so no one can find me.

GWEN STEFANI

Some days I feel like I should win best mom of the day award, and some days I find myself doing strange things that don't have any real purpose, in faraway corners in my house, and I realize I am literally and deliberately hiding from my children.

KATE HUDSON

When my kids become wild and unruly, I use a nice, safe playpen. When they're finished, I climb out.

ERMA BOMBECK

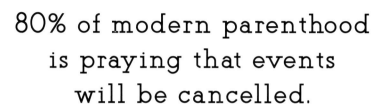

80% of modern parenthood is praying that events will be cancelled.

JENNIFER MENDELSOHN

section four

work hard,
mom hard,
it's all hard

I know stay-at-home moms
and I know career moms.
But I have yet to meet
a mom who doesn't work.

@MOMSTHEWORST

It's not difficult to take care of a child; it's difficult to do anything else while taking care of a child.

JULIANNE MOORE

You know you're a working mom when you walk into work with a chocolate thumbprint on your back from your goodbye hug.

HEATHER HENRY

I think every working mom probably feels the same thing: You go through big chunks of time where you're just thinking, 'This is impossible - oh, this is impossible.' And then you just keep going and keep going, and you sort of do the impossible.

TINA FEY

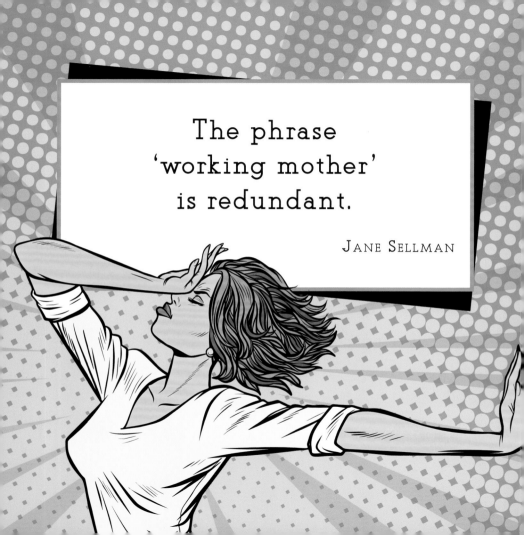

[wake up before everyone, shovel driveway, sanitize house, feed everyone, bring sick kid to doctor, bring her to pharmacy, bring her home, feed everyone again, shovel walkways, wash dishes, start laundry, settle kids at separate TVs, grab my laptop]

Me: OK, time to start my work!

KIM BONGIORNO

It is a well-known parenting fact that a toddler's overwhelming desire to 'do something themselves' is directly proportional to the number of minutes you are running late.

Love can change a person the way a parent can change a baby — awkwardly, and often with a great deal of mess.

LEMONY SNICKET

It's not easy being
a mother. If it were easy,
fathers would do it.

DOROTHY ON *THE GOLDEN GIRLS*

Me to baby: Say Dada!

Husband: You don't want her first word to be Mama?

Me: Hell no! The other two won't leave me alone. This one's yours.

STEPHANIE JANKOWSKI

[Married Pillow Talk]

Husband: Tell me what you want . . .

Me: I want you to take our kid to soccer practice tomorrow.

@PetrickSara

Me: are you ready?

Husband: yes

Me: great, I got myself and the kids ready and everything's packed up and we'll actually be on time if we leave right this second, let's get in the car-

Husband: okay, just need to hop in the shower real quick